Danny Dog

A rescue dog finds his forever home

Story by Sid Shapira

Illustrated by Izzy Bean

D1361517

Special thanks...

To my book editor, Simone Kaplan of Picture Book People,
for her candid and insightful feedback on the manuscript.

To my amazing wife, Sheryl Chesivoir, for her extraordinary
support, patience, and belief in this book.

Copyright © 2014 by Sid Shapira Communications

Printed in the United States of America

First Printing, 2014
ISBN 978-0-9906818-0-9

www.dannyrescuedog.com

This book is dedicated to Danny's late 'grandfather'
Daniel Chesivoir, whose spirit and zest for life
is reflected in his namesake.

To: Cole

Happy Reading!

Enjoy Danny's story!

(Danny's Dad)

Danny

Believe in Second Chances™

Saturdays were special for Samantha and Ethan.
It was their day with Grandma – shopping followed by a yummy lunch.
But, this Saturday would be different.

Outside the store, the children spotted an image in the distance.
Moving closer, Samantha shouted, "Are you lost?"
The little dog barked and sprinted toward them.
He was shivering as Samantha patted his damp, shaggy fur.

"He's so cute and he's all alone," said Ethan, as Grandma arrived. "And, he doesn't have a collar," said Samantha. "If he doesn't have a family, can we keep him? Please?"

"It's not that simple," said Grandma.
"Dogs need a yard and lots of attention.
We can't give him that."

"But, I have an idea," she said,
as she reached for her phone.
"I know someone who can help
find him a good home."

That afternoon, a pretty, golden-haired lady appeared at Grandma's door.

"My name is Gayle," said the lady. "I work for a pet rescue group."

"Are you going to find him a new family?" asked Ethan.

"I sure hope so," said Gayle.

Gayle gave the dog a collar, a leash, and a name – Jing Jing.
"We're going to a place where you'll be safe and warm," she told him.
"And, they'll give you a bath so you'll be clean and fresh."

Pet Rescue Center

As Gayle opened the door
to the red brick building,
a chorus of yelps and yaps
greeted them.

There were dogs of all shapes and sizes.
Some were big and some were small.
Some were short and some were tall.

Jing Jing was led to a cage that was filled with three blankets, a bowl of food, and water. It was better than wandering the streets, but it sure wasn't a home.

"I'll see you soon," said Gayle, as she gave him a big hug.

The little dog took walks in the morning
and played with the other dogs in the afternoon.
At night, he returned to his cage.
Every day was the same.

Everyone loved him.

"You are the cutest thing, Jing Jing," said Gayle.

"We'll find you a new home soon, I promise."

But, the days turned into weeks.
He wondered if he would ever find a new home.

Then one day, a well-dressed couple arrived to meet Jing Jing.
They decided to take him home.
The little dog darted toward their car.
He couldn't wait to see his new home.

From the car window, he saw children playing in a yard.
Could this be his new home?

The man gripped the leash tightly as they entered the house.
To Jing Jing's surprise, there was already a dog inside.

The other dog growled and grumbled and grunted.
He wanted nothing to do with the little dog in his house.

Then, he snarled and sneered at Jing Jing.
The man had to make a difficult decision.

"I'm sorry, Jing Jing, but we can't keep you," he said. "Our dog is used to getting all the attention. Now, he's upset. We must return you to the rescue center."

The little dog was heartbroken.
Would he ever find a family?
Was he meant to be a dog without a home?

He wanted more. He wanted to play in a yard.
He wanted to walk in a neighborhood.
And, he wanted to sleep in a real bed.

Jing Jing's spirits were down, but not for long.
A friendly couple appeared at the center looking to adopt a dog.

One glance at the little dog and they knew he was special.
Jing Jing dashed over and leaped into their arms.
Before long, the man smiled at him and said, "Let's go home."

The little dog hopped into the back seat,
then jumped into the driver's seat.
He pressed the buttons on the car door.
The windows rolled up and down.
"You're so playful," said his new mommy.
"You remind me of my dad. His name was Dan."
The little dog barked his approval.

"That's it," said his new daddy. "We'll call him Danny."
"Perfect," said mommy. "When we get home, Danny,
you'll meet your cat sisters."

Danny nervously approached the front door.
He remembered what happened the last time.
Inside, two cats with short, stubby tails greeted
him. They strolled up and started sniffing.
Danny wagged his tail.

"Winnie and Marley, meet Danny, your new brother," said mommy.

Danny began to chase Winnie and Marley all over the house.
Mommy and daddy couldn't stop smiling as they watched them play.

"We always wanted a dog and now we've found him," said daddy.
Danny grinned from ear to ear. At last, he had found his forever home.

from left: Marley, Sid, Winnie, Danny, and Sheryl

Danny Dog – A rescue dog finds his forever home is based on the true story of a lovable rescue dog – a 17-pound gray Shih Tzu – who entered our lives in 2013. The wonderful people from Emerald City Pet Rescue rescued Danny after he was found on the streets of Menifee, California.

We are indebted to them for bringing Danny into our lives.

A portion of the profit from this book will be donated to animal and human welfare organizations to help these nonprofits continue their dedicated and tireless work in the communities they serve.

We encourage all pet lovers to consider adopting rescue animals and giving them a second chance and a forever home.

– Sid & Sheryl

Emerald City Pet Rescue exists to rescue abused, neglected, and homeless animals from the streets and shelters from around the country, and sometimes abroad, and place them into loving and forever homes. Emerald City Pet Rescue is dedicated to offering its time and resources to house, train, rehabilitate, transport, and care for these animals. Emerald City Pet Rescue operates as a 501(c)(3) charitable organization.

For more information, visit: www.emeraldcitypetrescue.org.